MISSIONARY TRIUMPH OVER SLAVERY

MISSIONARY TRIUMPH OVER SLAVERY

William Knibb, and Jamaican Emancipation

PETER MASTERS

Drawn principally from the classic account by
Knibb's contemporary, John Howard Hinton

THE WAKEMAN TRUST, LONDON

MISSIONARY TRIUMPH OVER SLAVERY
© Peter Masters 2006

THE WAKEMAN TRUST
(Wakeman Trust is a UK Registered Charity)

UK Registered Office
38 Walcot Square
London SE11 4TZ

US Office
300 Artino Drive
Oberlin, OH 44074-1263
Web site: www.wakemantrust.org

ISBN   1 870855 53 1
ISBN-13 978 1 870855 53 2

Cover design by Andrew Owen
Featuring the British Fort at Port Antonio, Jamaica ©Iconotec

Printed by Stephens & George, Merthyr Tydfil, UK

EMANCIPATION TIMELINE

KING WILLIAM IV: 1765-1837 (reigned 1830-1837)

WILLIAM WILBERFORCE: 1759-1833

WILLIAM KNIBB: 1803-1845

ABOLITION OF SLAVERY ACT: August 28th, 1833
Britain abolishes slavery and provides for the emancipation
of enslaved people in the British West Indies, to take effect in
August 1834. The Act declares that the former enslaved people
must serve a period of apprenticeship before receiving full
emancipation. Originally this period was set at six years,
but it was later reduced to four.

EMANCIPATION DAY: August 1st, 1834

FULL EMANCIPATION: August 1st, 1838
Complete freedom granted throughout the British West Indies.
On the evening of July, 31st, 1838, the great chapel at
Falmouth, Jamaica was crowded an hour before midnight.
The closing hour of the last day of slavery
was passed in worship.

BEGINNING OF THE JAMAICAN AWAKENING: 1838

The Missionary Triumph
Over Slavery

I T IS OFTEN claimed that Christian missionaries since the early
1800s have been the servants and tools of imperialism, aiding
and abetting its oppressive ways in exchange for privileges and
protection. 'Political correctness' now puts missionaries in the dock
and charges them with being the worldwide murderers of liberty,
independence and culture. In the past this has been the charge levelled by communists, but more recently it has been taken up by
other plainly anti-Christian historians, and retailed by ill-informed
teachers in many British schools and colleges.

In its most virulent form, this charge has become a major part of
the onslaught against Christianity mounted by Islamic teachers in
their campaign for the hearts of young people whose forebears bore
the abuses of colonial oppression. This view of missionary work is,

however, a grotesque distortion of the truth, and 'historical revisionism' of the worst kind. Young people are being cheated of reality by those who want to discredit Christianity, portraying it as the white man's tool for bringing black colonies into submission.

It is true that the 'missions' of the 'Holy Roman Empire' were in the interests of imperialism. It is also true that much of the early work of Anglican clergy in British colonial territories was more for the benefit of the settlers, and not the indigenous population, and these clergy usually upheld colonial interests. But the great majority of Protestant missionaries went on a religious errand to win the souls of nationals, and nearly all found themselves despised, derided and opposed by their colonial authorities. As they worked to obtain spiritual conversions and to promote the educational and social advancement of the people, their greatest enemies were the white merchants and settlers, together with their sponsors, investors and parliamentary representatives in England.

Most of these missionaries were, at some time in their service, banned, arrested, molested, slandered and impeded by those whose ongoing power and wealth depended on the continuance of ignorance and slavery. Proof of the social and religious sincerity of most missionaries is to be seen in the alarmingly short life-span that they faced, most dying from local fevers within three years of arrival in their allotted region.

The subject of this book is an example of the majority of missionaries, and one whose battle against colonial outrages became legendary. William Knibb sailed with his wife, Mary, to Jamaica in 1824, aged only 21. Like most Baptist and Methodist missionaries they were years ahead of their time in their attitude to social liberty, and this brought upon them constant harassment from plantation and slave owners. But they held out, to win not only the souls of thousands, but their emancipation also.

William Knibb was by no means the first Baptist missionary to set foot in Jamaica, the first being George Lisle, a former slave from

Virginia who arrived in 1782 and founded a Baptist church in Kingston. The second was Moses Baker, a runaway slave from America who came to Christ under Lisle's preaching, later beginning a Baptist church in St James. These two wrote to Dr John Ryland Jnr, Principal of the Baptist Academy at Bristol, asking for missionaries. Dr Ryland (a co-founder with William Carey of the first British society for foreign missions) introduced the need to his students, and in 1814, John Rowe answered the call. He and his wife opened a school for the children of slaves, along with a Sunday School at Falmouth on the north coast of Jamaica, but before he could secure a licence for public preaching he died of yellow fever. At that time no Nonconformist missionary could preach in Jamaica without a licence from the Bishop of London, and the reluctant granting of this could take up to two years.

William Knibb was an energetic young man with a strong voice and a large heart. Born in Kettering, he was educated in the one-roomed town grammar school, and he learned the Gospel in the town's Calvinistic Baptist Sunday School. Later apprenticed to a Bristol printer, he professed conversion while attending the church pastored by Dr Ryland, and quickly set his heart on missionary service, following in the track of his elder brother.

Knibb proved his zeal for the Lord's work in many ways, including the leading of a mission in the poorest part of Bristol, where his intensive visitation and street preaching brought in numerous seekers in the span of a year. By the time Knibb arrived in Jamaica in 1824, six Baptist missionaries were already there. Knibb had volunteered to replace his elder brother, a missionary-schoolmaster, who had died at 23. With his wife, Knibb also would suffer much illness, both of them lying often at death's door, and suffering the loss of children. He was at first schoolmaster of the Baptist mission school at Kingston, which grew through his work to over 200 children, both slaves and free. Not content to be teaching six days a week, he opened a Sunday School also for adults and children.

Willliam Knibb as a young man

Soon after his arrival, he wrote home: 'The cursed blast of slavery has, like a pestilence, withered almost every moral bloom. I know not how any person can feel a union with such a monster, such a child of hell. I feel a burning hatred against it and look upon it as one of the most odious monsters that ever disgraced the earth. The iron hand of oppression daily endeavours to keep the slaves in the ignorance to which it has reduced them.'

Knibb could not stand the sight of people working on the treadmills and chain-gangs, nor the relentless whippings and floggings. 'Never argue,' he wrote, 'in support of a system so corrupt, so repugnant to every feeling of right and justice, and which must be viewed by God with total abhorrence. The moral degradation of the slaves is urged as a reason why they should not be freed. Their oppressors have reduced them so low that they can plead their condition as a reason for continued oppression! But let it not be thought that the slave is the only one who is vile. The white population is worse, far worse, than the victims of their injustice. There is scarcely a chaste person to be found.'

Within two years of his arrival, Knibb was to witness a resumption of frenzied opposition on the part of plantation owners to the work of the missionaries. When London overturned their attempts to legislate against missionary work (through the Jamaican House of Assembly) they turned to systematic slander to ruin the missionaries in the eyes of the authorities in London. Two missionaries were imprisoned, and Knibb was ordered by magistrates to stop preaching, which he refused to do.

The missionaries were then accused by the plantation owners of extorting money from their black congregations, stirring up the people by teaching equality and human rights, and encouraging prostitution to raise funds. These charges were published in a 'Sectarian Committee' report intended for wide circulation in England to encourage the government to pass anti-missionary laws, but it contained so many extreme and undocumented claims that its

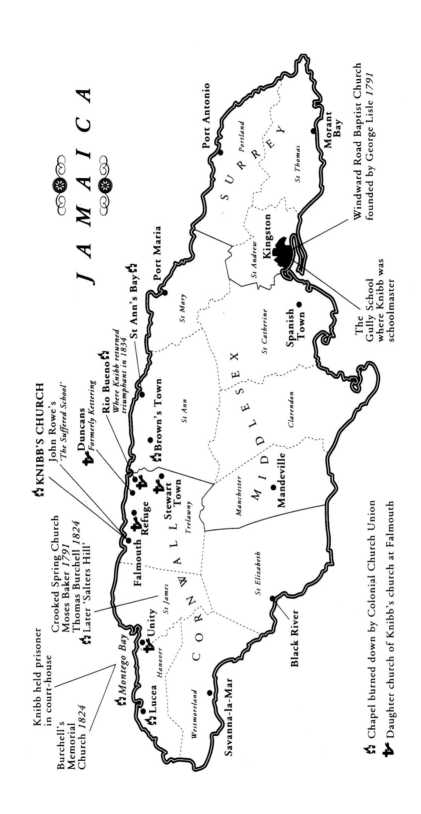

J A M A I C A

Port Antonio

Morant Bay

Windward Road Baptist Church
founded by George Lisle *1791*

Kingston

St Thomas

Portland

S U R R E Y

St Andrew

Port Maria

The
Gully School
where Knibb was
schoolmaster

St Mary

Spanish
Town

St Catherine

St Ann's Bay

Rio Bueno
*Where Knibb returned
triumphant in 1834*

Duncans
Formerly Kettering

KNIBB'S CHURCH
John Rowe's
'The Suffered School'

St Ann

Brown's Town

M I D D L E S E X

Crooked Spring Church
Moses Baker *1791*
Thomas Burchell *1824*
Later 'Salters Hill'

Clarendon

Manchester

Refuge

Stewart
Town

Trelawny

Mandeville

Falmouth

C O R N W A L L

St James

St Elizabeth

Black River

Montego Bay

Unity

Hanover

Lucea

Savanna-la-Mar

Westmoreland

Knibb held prisoner
in court-house

Burchell's
Memorial
Church *1824*

Chapel burned down by Colonial Church Union

Daughter church of Knibb's church at Falmouth

British representative refused to have anything to do with it.

Knibb moved from Kingston to Savanna-la-Mar in the west of Jamaica in 1828. From here, at the age of 26, he forwarded to England his account of the case of Sam Swiney:–

'An excellent young man of the name of Sam Swiney, a deacon of my church in this place, is now in chains for his love to Jesus. During my sickness he and others, both bond and free, met at my house to pray. Information of this was carried to the magistrates; and though I procured three respectable persons, neighbours, including the head constable, to prove on oath that no noise was made, which the informer had sworn to, the poor fellow was convicted.

'The magistrate would have it that preaching and praying were the same. I tried to convince him of the difference, but it was of no use; so for offering a prayer to God, and nothing more, this poor fellow is sentenced to receive twenty lashes on his bare back, and to be worked in chains on the roads for a fortnight.

'I did all I could to save him, and so did his owner, who told the magistrates that he had his permission. Next morning I went to see him flogged, determined to support him as well as I could, however painful to my feelings. There he was, a respectable tradesman, though a slave, stretched indecently on the ground, held firmly down by four slaves, two at his hands and two at his feet. The driver was merciful, or every lash would have fetched blood.

'He was raised from the ground, chained to a convict, and immediately sent to work. I walked by his side down the whole bay, to the no small annoyance of his persecutors. Amidst them I took him by the hand, told him to be of good cheer, and said, loud enough for them all to hear, "Sam, whatever you want, send to me and you shall have it." The good people here have behaved nobly to him, encouraging him by every means in their power; I shall see that he wants for nothing, and by my public notice of him show that I consider him a persecuted Christian.'

Knibb published an account of this in one of the island papers – a

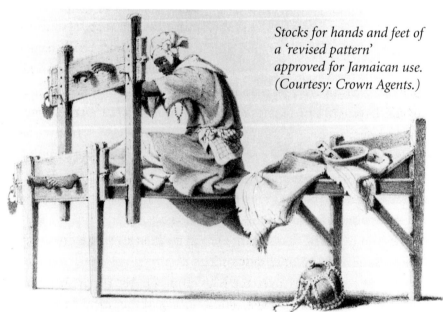

Stocks for hands and feet of a 'revised pattern' approved for Jamaican use. (Courtesy: Crown Agents.)

piece of unheard-of courage – for which he was threatened with a prosecution for libel. However, the affair excited so much sympathy in England that a sum of money was promptly raised by friends at Camberwell for the purchase of Sam Swiney's freedom. Knibb wrote home: 'Reproach and falsehood are plentifully bestowed upon me; but these, from their frequency, have long ceased to affect me. I procured the man's freedom, which was worth all.'

This, however, was not the only result of his involvement in the case of Sam Swiney. The English office of the mission forwarded his narrative to the Secretary of State for the Colonies, and he passed it to the Governor of Jamaica for investigation. Eventually the Secretary of State dismissed from office the two magistrates who had awarded the punishment for a gross abuse of power. But this only inflamed the fierce resentment of the Jamaican colonial authorities. The following year several of the missionaries were summoned to appear before the House of Assembly, which adopted a very menacing attitude towards them. The 'Consolidated Slave Law' of 1810-14 was re-enacted, designed to discourage rebellion among slaves. It prohibited the assembling of slave congregations 'between sunrise and sunset', banned the taking of offerings from slaves for Nonconformist work, and taxed the churches. The Jamaican authorities were determined to stop any teaching which dignified slaves and planted ideas in their minds 'above their station'. These measures would have virtually destroyed the work of the missionaries. 'I am determined,' wrote Knibb, 'not to obey the slave law, if it passes. The Methodists [also] are determined not to abide by the law.'

The spirit of the missionaries was fired, and the Lord blessed their labours. Knibb recorded: 'Notwithstanding all opposition, the work is proceeding gloriously. Thousands are flocking to hear the Word of God, and great numbers are joining themselves to the Lord. We are persecuted, but not in despair.'

In 1830 Knibb took over the 600-strong Baptist congregation at Falmouth on the north coast, already being well-known there from

Planting the sugar cane

his numerous preaching visits. The missionary who put Knibb's name to the congregation recorded that he had never seen such a positive response in his life. After proposing Knibb, he asked for a show of hands, and the entire membership stood, held up both hands and wept. The area teemed with sugar estates employing scores of thousands of slaves. Even Knibb, regarded as one of the strongest and hardest-working of the European missionaries of all denominations, found the work daunting and wrote: 'The *[preaching]* stations here are so numerous and so far apart that I know not how to supply my portion of them.' One of the churches visited by him involved an 86-mile return journey. Chapels had to be organised and built in many places where both slaves and free crowded to hear, but the looming insurrection was to cut into all these activities.

In 1831 a motion was brought before the British House of Commons for the gradual abolition of slavery in the British colonies. This was not immediately taken up by the government, although hope was expressed that future legislation would move to emancipation. The Jamaican planters were outraged at the prospect, denouncing abolition as insane and inhuman. The colonial overlords of the island met in various parishes to give vent to their anger and opposition to the drift of political opinion in England.

Jamaica was awash with angry conversation among the colonialists, most reacting with unrestrained fury, sometimes directed toward their slaves, and constantly in their hearing. The master of one slave told him that freedom was coming from England, but that he would shoot every slave rascal before it came. So slaves heard, through their masters, that the king intended to set them free, and that their masters were determined to prevent it. The information quickly spread to the slaves on the plantations, and soon the entire slave population became convinced that their masters would reject and resist the intentions of the king. The planters may fairly be said to have set their own estates on fire.

Knibb wrote anxiously, describing the state of high tension:–

Slaves v militia at Montpelier

'Such is the state of feeling here at present with respect to the extinction of slavery, that I should be almost afraid to go to any estate. I never knew anything like it, and in what it will end the Divine Being only knows. The slaves believe that they are soon to be free, and are anxiously waiting till King William sends them their free paper. Oppression and cruelty still go on. One of the inquirers here was this day threatened with flogging and imprisonment for not standing in the market all the Lord's Day to sell her master's goods. I went to the authority and prevented it, telling him plainly that I would send word to the Colonial Office if the woman was punished.'

Early in October several slaves came to Knibb as their minister to ask him if what they had heard was true, namely 'that the free paper was come'. Knibb's reply was, 'No, it is not true. When did busha tell you anything for your good?* There is no free paper coming. Go home, and mind your master's work.' At that time, however, he had no suspicion of a revolt, nor did his church members join in it.

As Christmas drew near, convinced that the king had made them free, it was suggested by a slave named Sam Sharpe that the slaves should not work after Christmas unless given wages. In order to unite slaves for this action, meetings were held by Sharpe on a plantation called 'Retrieve' from about the middle of October. The plan was developed in detail two weeks before Christmas. Sam Sharpe's schemes did not involve violent revolt, but some individuals went beyond his intentions and vowed to set fire to the properties and fight for freedom. By their acts the ultimate character of the revolt was decided. Soon, everything became known to the planters, who prepared to respond. From the missionaries, however, the plot had been concealed, their attitude against violence being too well-known for the more militant slaves to hope for their support. There was no

---

* Local white managers of plantations were known as 'bushas'.

Kingston militia returning from duty during the Jamaican insurrection. (Courtesy: Regent's Park College, Oxford.)

justification for the Baptist missionaries being blamed for the insurrection, but blamed they were.

On the night of 27th December the blaze of burning sugar-works signalled the start of the revolt and from that moment the authorities responded with military massacre and lawless revenge. Knibb heard of the intended revolt only the day before, and with other missionaries tried to convince the Christian congregations that the talk of freedom was untrue. Knibb was himself ordered to enlist in the colonial army as a private to help suppress the revolt, but almost at once he was arrested on suspicion of complicity. He wrote:–

'We were searched. When all was ready, we were paraded through the streets to the shore, guarded by four soldiers with a sergeant, and put into an open canoe. After a tedious voyage of seven hours, we were landed at Montego Bay about seven in the evening. The canoe being leaky, my feet were completely soaked; and this tended to increase the indisposition under which I was labouring. On landing we were marched to the court-house, then to headquarters, back to the court-house, then up a steep hill to the custos's [customs], then back to the court-house (which was made a barrack), where we were placed in the jury-box, under a guard of four soldiers.

'Every term of abuse that malice could invent was heaped upon us, with the most vulgar allusions that depraved nature could imagine. Twice was the bayonet pointed at my breast; and when I requested permission to lie down on the floor, being ill and having been harassed since the morning, I was damned and blasted, and told that if I moved I should be instantly shot. Value your privileges, Britons, and feel and pray for those poor Christian slaves who are entirely under the control of such beings. No pirate or savage Moor could have treated me worse than I was treated by Englishmen.

'No fault had I committed, but I was a missionary, and that was enough. I was thankful that I felt a disposition to pray for my enemies, who were taunting me that I should be shot on the morrow, and pleasing themselves with the sport.'

TO

THE REBELLIOUS SLAVES.

NEGROES,

YOU have taken up arms against your Masters, and have burnt and plundered their Houses and Buildings. Some wicked persons have told you that the King has made you free, and that your Masters withhold your freedom from you. In the name of the King, I come amongst you, to tell you that you are misled. I bring with me numerous Forces to punish the guilty, and all who are found with the Rebels will be put to death, without Mercy. You cannot resist the King's Troops. Surrender yourselves, and beg that your crime may be pardoned. All who yield themselves up at any Military Post *immediately*, provided they are not principals and chiefs in the burnings that have been committed, will receive His Majesty's gracious pardon. All who hold out, will meet with certain death.

WILLOUGHBY COTTON,
Maj. General Command⁹.

GOD SAVE THE KING.

Due to the intervention of two prominent colonialists, Knibb, with his fellow missionary sufferers, was given bail, while strenuous efforts were made by their persecutors to get up charges. Within a few hours of his removal from Falmouth, Knibb's house was searched by a magistrate, and papers taken. Great efforts were also made to obtain witnesses against him from among the slaves, but these failed. Three weeks passed as the work of military murder went on, and then an attempt was made to force Knibb to leave the island.

In the course of the mayhem and slaughter an Anglican clergyman named Bridges speedily formed an association of settlers called the 'Colonial Church Union'. Its aims were to oppose anti-slavery sentiments by a variety of means, including lobbying of the House of Assembly for the expulsion of all the Nonconformist missionaries, and the outlawing of any religious teaching other than that of the established English and Scottish churches.

The methods of the Colonial Church Union, taking advantage of the state of martial law, were those of terrorism. They formed groups of white planters to destroy the chapels. Baptist chapels fell in rapid succession – Salters Hill, Falmouth (which was Knibb's), Montego Bay, Rio Bueno, Brown's Town, Lucea and St Anne's Bay. Before the Governor could end this illegality, eleven Baptist churches (not to mention Methodist and Moravian places) were utterly gutted and pulled down. Missionaries of all societies left the island, but Knibb would not go.

When it became known that Knibb, still under arrest, was not prepared to be hounded out of Jamaica, the planters determined to take his life. Knibb was warned that they were on their way to where he was staying, armed with bludgeons. He took his family to the home of the only sympathetic member of the island's ruling body, who sheltered them, but Knibb himself was sent for his safety to a merchant ship in the harbour. He wrote:–

'I was taken prisoner on the charge of being concerned in the

Interior of a boiling house

rebellion that has broken out among the slaves. Although I have been five weeks in this state, or rather on bail, I do not know yet what the specific charges are. I know that I am innocent; but such is the awful state of feeling here, that my only hope of escape is in Him Who turneth the hearts of men as the rivers of water are turned. Should I escape, I shall return to England, as I am not safe from assassination in this part of the world.

'Our chapels at this place, at Falmouth, Rio Bueno, and I doubt not at other places, are levelled to the ground. Two days ago I escaped for my life, and took refuge on board one of His Majesty's ships in the harbour. I have this morning returned, being bound not to leave this place. My dear Mary is divinely supported under this deep trial, and has been of much comfort to me. The two children, William and Catharine, I have not seen for five weeks. Little Ann is with us, in ill health.

'I have been informed this morning, that the mob have destroyed, or intend to destroy, my books and furniture. I shall feel the loss of the books much, as I have striven hard for seven years to obtain them. The kindness of my thrice-dear people at Falmouth makes my heart overflow with gratitude to God: my heart is with them, but I fear that I shall never preach to them again. I look back on all the goodness and mercy which the Lord God has caused to pass before me. Seven years ago I landed on this island, and do I repent coming? No! With eternity and a jail in prospect, I do not.

'I mourn over my sins, I long to be more active in the service of God, and earnestly do I pray that I may come forth from the furnace of affliction purified as gold seven times tried. Brother Burchell is taken as a prisoner on shore. Heard the painful news that both he and dear Gardner are committed to jail; may God support them.'

A little later he wrote:–

'It is now six weeks since I have been permitted to preach the Gospel. Often do I think of my dear people in Falmouth; their kindness overwhelms me. The chapel is razed to the ground, and they are

Crop-time on a sugar estate. 'Canefields.'

scattered as sheep without a shepherd. Mrs K. went to Falmouth to look after the furniture saved from the infuriated whites by our female friends, the Lord in His mercy protect her! In the evening heard that I was released from my bail, having been a prisoner seven weeks, and not any charge brought against me. Heard that they were trying to find one; may the Lord disappoint them, if it be His will.'

Having been released from custody at Montego Bay, Knibb went to Falmouth. Here he found the white residents in a murderous state of mind, and his landlord told him not to return as he dared not rent to him. Knibb accepted lodging at the house of a free black Jamaican. His furniture had been saved from destruction only by the promptness of his friends in removing it. His chapel had been destroyed after having been used during the insurrection as barracks for a regiment of militia.

Two men informed him that a party had assembled for the purpose of murdering him, and warned him especially against going out in the evening. They also warned him of an intention to attack the house and to tar and feather him, and this was actually attempted. For three successive nights a group of 50 white planters stoned his lodging, and he had to escape by day for the sake of his host. A further effort was made to arrest and charge Knibb, but this also failed for lack of credible witnesses. But the malignant spirit of the white population continued to threaten his life.

During this turbulent period in Jamaica, which is termed 'the reign of terror', it was impossible for slaves on the various estates who were members of Knibb's congregation to give any sign of their sympathy with him. Nevertheless, when they were wrongly told that Knibb had been executed, their deep concern for him was obvious, and when he returned to Falmouth, messengers came from thirty estates to see if this was true.

In 1832 the oppressed Baptist community of Jamaica decided to send Knibb to England to plead their cause, so at 29, the persecuted missionary became 'Jamaica's advocate'. Once home, he embarked

The notorious treadmill was on all the Jamaican estates. (Courtesy: Regent's Park College, Oxford.)

on a most extensive and gruelling tour of churches throughout Scotland and England, telling in public meetings of the work of the Gospel and of the oppression of the slaves. Almost single-handedly he swept from the minds of many thousands of people any lingering susceptibility to the lies and half-truths of colonial self-justification, and his message spread throughout Nonconformity.

Knibb's public addresses had a power altogether overwhelming. Sceptics were convinced, waverers became decided, apathetic people were roused, and great numbers of hearts everywhere kindled to irrepressible support. With perhaps a single exception, the eloquence of no one man made a larger or more distinguished contribution to the change of public opinion. British colonial slavery at last really began to cower and fall.

It was not, however, by his public meetings alone that Knibb forwarded the anti-slavery cause. In the session of 1832, committees were appointed in both Houses of Parliament to inquire into the state of the West Indian colonies. These committees were sitting when Knibb arrived in England, and he was summoned to appear before them. He was examined by the House of Commons' committee for four days, and by the Lords' for three. No one can study the record of these examinations without noting their searching character, and the way in which everything was done to discredit his testimony. Knibb's evidence, however, was so authentic and unassailable that it contributed more than that of any other witness to the conviction of all, that slavery must be speedily abolished.

In the course of Knibb's examination before the committee of the House of Lords he had exposed the gross immoralities committed on many of the estates, stating that very frequently these were promoted by the managers of the properties, commenting that some noble lords could be little aware what was going on upon their own West Indies holdings. On his appearing in the lobby the next day, he was sent for by the Earl of Harewood, who said: 'Mr Knibb, I have been quite distressed by the account you gave us of what was going

The Exeter Hall in the Strand, London (later used by Spurgeon prior to the opening of the Metropolitan Tabernacle), filled for meetings addressed by Knibb during 1832. British Nonconformists rallied to his support. (Courtesy: Regent's Park College, Oxford.)

on upon some of our estates. Be frank with me. Is that the state of things on my estate? If you say it is, I will by the next mail direct the removal of my manager, but he shall never know that it is in consequence of information received from you.'

Knibb informed the peer that it was not the case on his estate, and his lordship replied, 'Give me your hand, and make me this promise, that if, when you return, you find anything of the kind going on upon my estate you will immediately inform me. I shall recognise your initials, W. K., that will be quite enough, and I will act upon it immediately.'

It is especially interesting to note that although Knibb did his utmost to protect slaves in Jamaica, and to arouse public meetings and Parliament while in Britain, he would never incite slaves to rebellion, nor even mention to them his burning desire for their freedom. He set out to change the law, if he could, but taught that it should be obeyed while it stood. Superficial and critical writers today seize on this aspect of missionary policy, using it as the basis of their charge that missionaries supported the colonial power. They make no reference to the labours of Knibb and others to end slavery, nor to their own suffering at the hands of the local colonial government, nor to their Herculean efforts to guide slaves, once emancipated, to prove their capacity to handle freedom.

Knibb was interrogated at length by the Commons' committee about the substance and manner of his preaching to the slaves. The report of his questioning includes the following:–

Q. 'What were the doctrines bearing on the temporal condition of the black population, which you inculcated?

A. – I never touched upon the subject in my life.

Q. 'In preaching to the slave population, have you not found it very difficult to keep separate the spiritual concerns of that black population from their temporal situations?

A. – It is difficult, but every good man would do it.

Q. 'Is it possible, in addressing an unlettered audience, in inculcating the doctrine of the freedom of the faith of Christianity, not to expose yourself to misinterpretation as to temporal freedom, as contrasted with spiritual freedom?

A. – Whenever I have had occasion to speak on that subject, I have explained, that when freedom is mentioned in the Word of God, it referred to the soul and not to the body; that there were slaves in the times of the apostles as well as at present.

Q. 'In preaching you have touched on this subject?

A. – On spiritual subjects I have preached the whole counsel of God.

NEGRO APPRENTICES.

At a PUBLIC MEETING
OF THE BIRMINGHAM
ANTI-SLAVERY
SOCIETY,

Held the 12th. of September, 1836.   It was unanimously Resolved,
THAT a Copy of the Reports of Corporal Punishments inflicted on the
Apprenticed Negroes of Jamaica, by the Special Justices of that Colony, in the
months of April, May, and June last, furnished by **THEMSELVES**, be published
and placarded on the walls of Birmingham.

FLOGGING
BY ORDER OF
Special Magistrates.

	1836. April	May.	June.	Total Number.		1836. April	May.	June.	Total Number.
Alley, W H	—	37	—	37	Hulme, J R	25	24	127	176
Baines T J	—	40	176	216	Jones Thomas W	35	44	130	209
Baynes E D	167	39	418	624	Kelley D W	25	—	20	45
Bell W A	40	110	32	182	Kent Henry	—	20	—	20
Bourne Stephen	10	20	39	69	Laidlan Henry	55	28	15	98
Brownson W H	—	—	25	25	Lambert R S	188	164	272	624
Carnaby William	50	40	35	125	Lloyd Samuel	21	142	382	545
Chamberlayne R. jun.	20	—	—	20	Lyon Edmund B	89	—	—	89
Cocking Ralph	78	—	117	195	Marlton W F	77	30	20	127
Cooper Richard S	—	—	39	39	M'Leod A N				
Daughtrey John	45	—	12	57	Moresby, Henry	359	690	472	1521
Davies Thomas	126	36	78	240	Nolan, James	35	—	40	75
Dawson J K	30	—	138	168	Odell, John	50	30	40	120
Dawson H W	—	—	25	25	Oliver, T. M.	140	175	200	515
Dillon T A	60	255	197	512	Palmer, A. L.	24	—	—	24
Dunne Patrick	30	—	—	30	Pennell, R. C.	60	391	400	851
Ewart David	—	—	—		Philip, E. D.	80	20	110	210
Facey Richard B	—	55	—	55	Pryce, Samuel	—	125	227	352
Finlayson Walter	20	—	50	70	Ramsay, William				
Fishbourne E E	120	260	265	645	Rawlinson, S.	219	25	250	494
Fyfe Alex. Gordon	9	20	—	29	Reynolds, John				
Gregg G D	—	48	180	228	Rennell, Robert				
Gurley John	30	—	30	60	Sowley, W. H	271	210	462	943
Grant J W	—	30	—	30	St. John, Richard	264	319	598	1181
Gordon George	4	39	—	63	Thomas, J R	567	230	296	1093
Hamilton Chenney	5	20	15	40	Thompson, R	—	—	51	51
Harris James	233	57	102	392	Waddington, H	78	36	210	324
Hawkins Charles	140	74	126	340	Walsh, H	82	25	12	119
Higgins G O	—	—	—		Welsh, Arthur	18	123	87	228
Hill Richard	—	—	—		Willis, George	99	40	20	159
Hewitt William	24	—	304	328	Woolfreys, John				
						4122	4071	6834	15037

**This does not include the secret flogging, the tortures on the Tread Mill,
the robbery of the Negro of his time, &c. &c. which there is a moral certainty exists
to a fearful extent, though kept from public view.**

B. HUDSON, PRINTER, BULL-STREET.

Q. 'Part of which is the freedom of the Christian?

A. – Yes, the spiritual freedom; but it has been very seldom that I have touched on that point; I have never preached a set sermon on that; certainly I should not keep back anything in the Word of God.

Q. 'Thinking it your duty to preach the whole counsel of God, part of which you know is the freedom of the Christian in matters of faith, do you not think you must have been exposed to misconception on the part of an unlettered audience, confounding spiritual with temporal freedom; do not you think it natural, or not impossible?

A. – I think the manner in which my congregation acted is a sufficient proof that they did not misunderstand it.

Q. 'Have you at all times been most guarded in the selection of the topics upon which you have preached to them?

A. – I have. It is rather delicate for me to speak of myself; but I think if I had not, the efforts that have been made to incriminate me would not have failed. I had one hundred and thirty witnesses, and I stand ready at any moment in Jamaica, to produce one thousand slaves to prove the nature of my instructions.

Q. 'You have said you thought it your duty to preach the whole counsel of God; is there not a text of this sort, "The truth shall make you free"?

A. – Yes, of that nature; but I never preached from it, nor would I preach from it, because the same doctrine might be conveyed from other texts. I never did quote such a passage of Scripture in addressing a slave congregation.

Q. 'Did you find it necessary to abstain from quoting particular passages of Scripture for the purpose of avoiding the exciting of any undue feeling in the mind of the Negro on the subject of liberty?

A. – I thought it my duty to do so.

Q. 'As the slaves who can read having access to the Scriptures would naturally find passages of that description, did they never come to you to ask you questions on passages of that kind?

A crowded market place

A. – They never did.

Q. 'No inquiries were made with regard to passages of that kind, which occur frequently in the Holy Scriptures?

A. – No; whenever we received a member in the church we always enforced the duty of obedience to masters, which would lead them to suppose that we considered slavery quite compatible with Christianity.'

Soon after these hearings, Knibb wrote the following to a missionary in Jamaica:–

'You can scarcely conceive the efforts that some are making to implicate us in the late rebellion, or the falsehoods which are placarded through the streets against us. I have already travelled more than 1,300 miles, and have to preach and speak almost every evening. I have been pleading the cause of our poor members in every town where I have been able to speak, and cannot but think it a mercy that I came to England, though I frequently wish the burden had fallen on abler hands. The people in this land are determined to have the system down. I think if something is not done immediately, it will be *demanded*. The conduct of the whites in Jamaica is viewed by all who are not interested in upholding the accursed system with unmingled disgust.'

For all his noted vigour and ceaseless activity, Knibb was frequently overtaken by very deep spasms of depression, a trial reflected in this passage from a letter to his wife:

'I preached twice on the Sabbath in Edinburgh. In the morning I felt very wretched, and could not preach from the subject I had chosen. I took another while the congregation were singing the second hymn, and my heavenly Father assisted me, though I was so ashamed that I scarce dared look anyone in the face.

'In the afternoon one of the deacons, a very good man, came and told me how much they were gratified, and that they had voted £5 to the mission as a token of their approbation. Thus was God better than my fears. I preached in the evening in the largest place I have ever seen. It was crowded to excess, 2,500 being present. The Lord

THE REV. WILLIAM KNIBB,
WITH A LANDSCAPE OF THE MISSION CHAPEL AND GROUN JAMAICA.
SIGNED, ENGRAVED, AND PRINTED BY G. BAXTER, PATENTEE   COLOUR PRINTING.

Knibb in 'later life' with a landscape of the mission chapel and grounds.
On his lap is a volume of the Scriptures which he translated into the
Jamaican vernacular, on the table the proclamation abolishing slavery.
The original is in the National Portrait Gallery.
(Courtesy: Regent's Park College, Oxford.)

was with me, I hope.'

The parliamentary session of 1833 was at last distinguished by the achievement of the awaited legislative measure – the act for the abolition of British colonial slavery. Knibb subsequently addressed the annual meeting of his missionary society saying –

'No one but myself knows with what agitated feelings I stood before you at your last anniversary. After much prayer, I felt that, if I did not come forward in the way I then proposed, I should not be happy on my dying pillow. Feeling as I did the rights of the Negro, his capacity for improvement, and his steady attachment to the truths of the Gospel under heavy persecution, I felt bound to assert his claim to immediate emancipation. I had seen the sufferings and heard the groans of the oppressed; I was satisfied that the Christian world alone could relieve them; and I came to ask for that relief. I rejoice that in one short year so much has been accomplished.

'Having now come with you to the tomb of colonial slavery, I desire to bury every grain of animosity to the planter in the same grave with the system itself. Christians, with uplifted hands and voices, may now exclaim, "Ashes to ashes, and dust to dust!" '

Later, Knibb recalled this episode in his life. 'I was forced from the den of infamy and from a gloomy prison, with my congregation scattered, many of the members of my church murdered, and multitudes of the faithful lashed. I came home and I shall never forget the three years of struggle, and the incessant anxiety upon my spirit as I passed through the length and breadth of the country detailing the slaves' wrongs.'

William Wilberforce died a month before the abolition bill became law, and did not see the fruit of his long toil. The legislation set the date for the termination of slavery as 1st August 1834, but it required slaves to undergo six years of apprenticeship to prepare them for full freedom. This provision, however, was so ruthlessly abused by the planters that further campaigning secured the early granting of full freedom in 1838.

Falmouth, around 1840. (Courtesy: Regent's Park College, Oxford.)

Knibb returned to Jamaica in 1834 with a large sum of money he had won from the British government, supplemented by donations from churches, given for the rebuilding of churches destroyed by planters. He had been forced to leave his Falmouth congregation of 885 people with only their ruined building, but with help from another missionary they had regathered and grown, so that just before Knibb's return 1,600 people attended a series of emancipation thanksgiving services held in a huge shed.

When Knibb resumed his work in Jamaica he had to face the planters whose system of supremacy had been wrested from them. They had driven him to England and there he had struck a decisive blow at their power. They had 'flung the firebrand out of their hearths, and it had fallen on the powder magazine'. He had fought them on the ground *they* had chosen, and now returned as their conqueror.

Of his arrival, Knibb wrote:–

'As soon as the boat could be made seaworthy we embarked for Rio Bueno *[about 17 miles east of Falmouth]*, which we reached in safety the same evening. On entering this lovely little bay the first object that attracted my attention was the ruins of the chapel in which I had many times proclaimed the words of eternal life. There they stand, a monument to the shame of Jamaica's slave-drivers.

'But the person who set fire to the chapel is beneath the clods of the valley. Shortly after this transaction he left his home for a ride, was missed for two days, and was then accidentally discovered by a Negro, hanging between two rocks, quite mad. He was carried home, and he died in the same state.

'The people saw me as I stood on the deck of the boat. As I neared the shore I waved my hand, and they, being fully assured that it was their minister, ran from every part of the bay to the wharf. Some pushed off in a canoe, into which I got, with my family, and soon landed on the beach. We were nearly pushed into the sea by kindness. Poor Mrs K. was quite overcome. They took me up in their arms, they sang, they laughed, they wept, and I wept too. "Him come, him come, for true . . . King Knibb. Him fight the battle, him win the crown." On they rushed to the chapel, where we knelt together at the throne of mercy.

'On the following morning we started by land for Falmouth. The poor people in the pass all knew me, and had I stopped to shake hands with all, I should have been long on the road. As I entered Falmouth I could scarcely contain my feelings; nor can I now. I was, and am, completely overcome. They stood, they looked. "It him, it him for true. But see how him stand! Him make two of what him was when him left."

'Soon the news spread, and from twenty to twenty-five miles' distance they came. In the evening we had a prayer-meeting, and the chapel was crowded. As I set my foot on the threshold they struck up unexpectedly,

> Kindred in Christ, for His dear sake,
> A hearty welcome here receive:
> May we together now partake,
> The joys which only He can give.
> (John Newton)

'On the Sabbath day, when the people could come from the country, the scene was the most interesting I ever beheld. At six in the morning the place was full; at the ten o'clock service numbers were on the outside. The magistrates were present. I preached as well as my feelings would allow, and afterwards I addressed the people on the change in their circumstances. O the happiness of having the tongue set free from the shackles of slavery! I am sure you will excuse my feelings. It was such a noble sight! They were as still as death. I urged upon them the duties they would have to perform, and told them I was sure they would fulfil.'

For years the extreme abuse directed toward Knibb by the planters and their newspapers would continue, but the attitude of some officials mellowed, and when the rebuilt Falmouth church was almost completed, the congregation were freely given Sunday facilities in the court-house where Knibb had previously been held prisoner. By this time (1837) the congregation had grown to 1,800, and a very large chapel with deep galleries was required, not to mention accommodation for crowds of Sunday School children.

When Knibb had first gone to Jamaica, he had submitted to his missionary society's policy of silence on the matter of slavery, because the Gospel and not social reform was the chief purpose of their work. In England, however, he was not bound by that policy, and so he became the unshackled advocate of freedom. With the law now clear, he returned to Jamaica uninhibited in his outspokenness against oppression. When *local* laws passed by the Jamaican Assembly sought to thwart and dilute the purposes of the British Parliament's abolition act, he exposed their illegality and opposed them. On one occasion he appealed to the Governor, the Marquis of Sligo, to stop the illegal flogging of people by a treadmill supervisor, and this action resulted in the prosecution of that brutal individual.

The free members of his own church who owned 'slaves' (now technically 'apprentices') all resolved to set them free soon after the opening of the new chapel. The new freedoms of these apprentices were 'bestowed' in a public service which attracted great attention, but which further angered the planters.

When the apprenticeship system ('semi-slavery') was ended in 1838, countless slaves who had been prevented from attending churches were now free to do as they pleased. They flocked to hear the missionaries, and vast numbers were moved to repentance and faith. At the end of one Sunday, Knibb wrote: 'Today I baptised 75 persons and 1,300 sat down to the Lord's Supper. It was one of the happiest days of my life.'

Knibb now gained a new burden – that of teaching and educating thousands of children who were newly free, and to whom missionaries had previously had no access. 'What to do I know not. I could at once establish full six more day schools, if I had but the means. I

A Jamaican baptism held at the time of Knibb. (Courtesy: Regent's Park College, Oxford.)

have young men ready, and the desire for instruction is now greater than ever it was. Thousands of poor, long-neglected children, who at six years old were made apprentices, but who will now be free, earnestly desire it.

'O how ardently I long to feed these lambs! But I cannot. To behold mental misery longing to be relieved, and to be unable to impart the relief, is to me most distressing. Think, that all the labouring population of six years old were bound to work for their owners. To them, except on the Sabbath, we had no method of giving instruction. In eight weeks, blessed be God, they will all be free. These are to form the first free peasantry. How important that they should be at once instructed!'

The pro-slavery press in Jamaica continued to attack Knibb. One series of articles claimed that his church members regularly stole money in order to supply his demands. On one occasion the town of Falmouth was covered with posters bearing claims that Knibb 'the Baptist parson' had in his youth illegally run away from his apprenticeship to a baker and later been sacked from a coach-driving job for drunkenness. He then, it was claimed, had turned religious, but was rejected by his church for wicked behaviour.

Such trials however were light to missionaries whose lives were often so short. In the year after Knibb's return to Jamaica eight missionaries died of yellow fever or cholera. At 35, he wrote: 'I cannot expect much longer to labour for I have lived longer in Jamaica than most missionaries do.'

Jamaican missionaries laboured among believers who bore the deep scars of slavery. Uneducated and institutionalised, their degree of dependence upon their pastors, once freedom came, was at first almost total. It fell to the missionaries to lead them socially as well as spiritually, and to find ways of providing what years of oppression had withheld. Knibb explained the position to a home-mission officer who could not grasp why the missionaries were so involved with the general lives of the people:–

A settlement of freed slaves

'Here we are obliged to be everything religiously, politically, civilly, and (if I may coin a word) *buildingly*. While our brethren at home have deacons who can manage the temporal affairs of the church and collect the necessary moneys, we must be responsible for all, and manage all. At home there are laymen to whom people may go for advice, even for legal advice, but here, *ours* is the only appeal. Every disagreement, domestic or civil, comes before us. By our advice they go to law, or by our advice abstain. It is just the same in political matters; not a step will they take, nor an agreement will they sign, without asking us. Often I have had persons come to me for advice who have walked twenty miles to ask it.

'All their *[legal]* titles are brought to us to see if they are right (and the knowledge that this will be done prevents many attempts at gross oppression). Thus, after the morning is past, a missionary is not sure of an hour *[for his own labours]*. Now what are we to do? If we do not do these things they will not be done at all. And if ever, pressed out of measure, you say, "Really you must go to the magistrate, I cannot attend to it," then the cry is, "Minister, who but you will tell me what to do?" So on we go, and prevent as much mischief as we can.

'You need not be afraid of political action in Jamaica. In fact there is none. The words Whig and Tory are here unknown. There is not that love of country there ought to be, and Jamaica is sinking under an apathetic feeling which acquiesces in everything her rulers propound, however absurd, or however injurious.

'A few needy adventurers and unprincipled lawyers are our members *[of the House of Assembly]*, who, free from arrest, defy law and laugh at honesty. The infamy of their private character is in perfect keeping with their political degeneracy; and it was *our* rulers and their admirers that Sir Lionel Smith had in view, when he said, with just severity, "Jamaica is composed of white savages, and black Christians." '

Besides the work of the Gospel, therefore, the missionaries now

Crop-time on a sugar estate. 'Mill yard.'

had to train former slaves to cope with free employment, negotiation of fair wages and terms, cultivation of ground, and the handling of money. They also taught them to manage without the free provisions which slavery had given them. In this way the missionaries helped deprive the planters of their hoped for 'vindication' when ex-slaves proved incapable of the responsibilities of freedom.

The seven years following 1838 – the dawn of *full* freedom – proved to be years of quite astonishing spiritual harvest, for now there came the great season of Jamaican awakening. Baptists, Methodists, Moravians and Presbyterians were all mightily instrumental, but the Baptist missionaries and chapels were the most numerous, and they undoubtedly saw the greatest fruit of this glorious fire of the Lord. Baptists, with all their Calvinistic care and concern to see a real work of God in hearts, did not receive new members easily, and yet the people came, wept, and clung to Christ, repenting and believing with all their hearts.

Amazingly, the vice, degradation and deep scars of slavery were lifted from many thousands of seemingly hopeless lives, and a new nature given in exchange. One of the most remarkable statistical tables in the history of awakenings illustrates the scale of blessing, and its moral results, during the post-insurrection years in Jamaica. Twelve years before 1845, in one particular region of Jamaica (Westmoreland, in the extreme west) there could not be found any couple properly married, such was the degradation encouraged within slavery, and this reflected the moral chaos prevalent throughout the island. But between the years 1842-44 alone, the registered marriages for the whole of Jamaica were recorded as follows:–

Baptists – 8,710 couples

Anglicans – 8,294 couples

Methodists – 5,580 couples

Moravians – 2,839 couples

Presbyterians – 2,382 couples

Congregationalists – 554 couples

Roman Catholics – 3 couples

Total – 28,362 marriages.

It could truly be said that 'the floodgates of licentiousness were closed,' and 'morality and virtue now stand where immorality and vice prevailed.'

Speaking of the seven years after the granting of full freedom, Knibb wrote: 'In the midst of these scenes the work of mercy extended so that in those seven years, through the labour of about twenty missionaries, 22,000 people were baptised upon their profession of faith in Jesus Christ.'

During Knibb's fourth visit to England in 1845, he was able to provide the following statistics about the growth of the Baptist work. In the years since their buildings were all destroyed by white hostilities, 47 new chapels had been built and many new schoolrooms. Many of the churches had achieved financial independence in the support of their own missionary pastor, and the greater share of the cost of the buildings had been met by local giving from former slaves.

Knibb's own church at Falmouth (which now seated 2,500) had grown during ten years from 650 to 1,280 members. During this time over 3,000 people had been baptised and admitted to membership, but some 2,050 had been sent to form other churches. Others had, of course, died. It is striking that only 100 had, over these years, been put out of fellowship through non-attendance or sinful behaviour. Six daughter churches were started by the Falmouth church, Refuge being the first such child (with 780 members), Rio Bueno the next (315 members), then Waldensia (746), Stewart Town (814), Unity (340) and finally Kettering, named after Knibb's birthplace (200).

When Knibb returned to Jamaica (aged 42) for what were to be the closing months of his life, there were extraordinary scenes of appreciation. He arrived at Falmouth, Jamaica on the evening of the

1st August. No sooner was his arrival known than preparations were made for a grand demonstration of public feeling to be held three days later.

Mrs Knibb, in a letter, later wrote of 'the tumultuous rejoicings' of that day. 'The procession,' she recorded, 'was more than a mile long, on a road as wide as any road I have seen in England. It commenced at a free township called Granville [after Granville Sharp], and was said to contain more than a thousand horses, and twenty different kinds of carriage. On the long line of road we could see nothing but a forest of heads. My dear husband, I know, felt gratified – he must have done so – for people had come from all parts to welcome his return.'

This great multitude, with various banners held aloft, moved in grand procession into Falmouth, loudly cheering as they passed the different estates, and pausing in front of the Baptist chapel. As many as could get into this building entered, and the crowds who could not, dispersed.

Now that Knibb had returned, his old enemies the white planters were bent upon punishing him in a different way. 'The Jamaican press,' he wrote, 'is full of rancour, quite as much as when I advocated the abolition of slavery. What they are not going to do with me when the House of Assembly meets it is hard to say, and certainly I do not care.'

Knibb's end came very suddenly, as was so often the case with the Jamaican missionaries of those days. One day he was all activity, the next sickness struck. He baptised 42 villagers at a Sunday morning service, making touching and solemn remarks over each person. He preached his last sermon the same evening from *1 Timothy 1.11*, and walked home. He travelled to Kettering the following day to minister and visit homes, but by Tuesday was very unwell. On the Wednesday 'typhoid fever' came on, and by Friday 'yellow fever of the most malignant character', which ended his life the following day. Delirium commenced within hours of the end – 'then black

An old photograph of Knibb's tomb outside the church at
Falmouth, Jamaica. The inscription reads:

'To the memory of William Knibb,
who departed this life at Kettering, Trelawny on the
15th Nov 1845 in the 43rd year of his age.

'This monument was erected by the emancipated slaves
to whose enfranchisement and elevation his indefatigable
exertions so largely contributed; by his fellow labourers who
admired and loved him, and deeply deplore his early removal; and
by friends of various creeds and parties, as an expression of their esteem
for one whose praise as a man, a philanthropist, and
a Christian minister, is in all the churches,
and who, being dead, yet speaketh.'

vomit, the certain harbinger of death'.

On the evening before his death, though very weak, he sang a hymn, offered a cogent and tender prayer, and gently dismissed those around his bed with the words, 'The service is over; you may go.' From that moment he lapsed into semi-consciousness, uttering only a few coherent sentences, including the words, 'All is well!'

Then another missionary champion of the oppressed went home to be with the Lord. A great servant of the Lord had run his race, first as a winner of souls, secondly as a pastor-teacher, and thirdly as a man who could never be bribed or subverted by the overtures of colonial oppressors. 8,000 people are said to have crowded to Knibb's funeral at Falmouth, Jamaica, his burial place. His wife Mary lived on for 25 years, labouring for the Lord in Jamaica, and dying at Waldensia.

William Knibb, above all, was an evangelist. A true lover of lost souls, he was a child of that wonderful and long season of church history, when Calvinists were activists and soul-winners, and when young men proved themselves for the Gospel ministry by street preaching and ragged-school evangelism. Knibb learned his missionary zeal in that golden age, believing that a missionary should never stand still. To such labourers the Lord came down in sovereign mercy and touched their lips to preach an irresistible call of mercy.

Men of Purpose

157 pages, illustrated, paperback, ISBN 1 870855 41 8

This book brings into one illustrated volume eleven great lives, all with an experience of personal conversion to God. Composer Mendelssohn, food industrialist Henry Heinz, novelist Daniel Defoe, and some of the most celebrated scientists of all time, are among the examples of leading people whose lives were changed by a sight of real Christianity.

Also very suitable as a gift to unconverted friends, and to enrich sermons and Bible class messages.

> The Dawn of Electricity – Michael Faraday
> Founder of a Food Empire – Henry J. Heinz
> A Composer's Journey – Felix Mendelssohn
> The 'Lord Apostol' – Lord Radstock
> Genius at Work – James Clerk Maxwell
> The Heart of a Hymnwriter – Philip P. Bliss
> Ex-Brewery Heir – Fred Charrington
> Spearhead into the Unknown – Lord Kelvin
> The Prodigal Poet – James Montgomery
> Pioneer of Power – Sir John Ambrose Fleming
> Father of Modern Journalism – Daniel Defoe

Faith, Doubts, Trials and Assurance

139 pages, paperback, ISBN 1 870855 50 7

Ongoing faith is essential for answered prayer, effective service, spiritual stability and real communion with God. In this book many questions are answered about faith, such as –

How may we assess the state of our faith? How can faith be strengthened? What are the most dangerous doubts? How should difficult doubts be handled? What is the biblical attitude to trials? How can we tell if troubles are intended to chastise or to refine? What can be done to obtain assurance? What are the sources of assurance? Can a believer commit the unpardonable sin? Exactly how is the Lord's presence felt?

Dr Masters provides answers, with much pastoral advice, drawing on Scripture throughout.

Heritage of Evidence

127 pages, illustrated, paperback, ISBN 1 870855 39 6

In today's atheistic climate most people have no idea how much powerful evidence exists for the literal accuracy and authenticity of the biblical record. The British Museum holds a huge number of major discoveries that provide direct corroboration and background confirmation for an immense sweep of Bible history. This survey of Bible-authenticating exhibits has been designed as a guide for visitors, and also to give pleasure and interest to readers unable to tour the galleries. It will also be most suitable for people who need to see the accuracy and inspiration of the Bible.

The 'tour' followed here started life over forty years ago and has been used by many thousands of people including youth and student groups.

Almost every item viewed on the tour receives a full colour photograph. Room plans are provided for every gallery visited showing the precise location of artefacts, and time-charts relate the items to contemporary kings and prophets. The book is enriched by pictures and descriptions of famous 'proofs' in other museums.

God's Rules for Holiness
Unlocking the Ten Commandments
139 pages, paperback, ISBN 1 870855 37 X

The Lord's Pattern for Prayer
Studying the lessons and spiritual encouragements
in the most famous of all prayers
118 pages, paperback, ISBN 1 870855 36 1

Joshua's Conquest
Was it moral? What does it say to us today?
119 pages, paperback, ISBN 1 870855 46 9

The Mutual Love of Christ and His People
An explanation of the *Song of Solomon* for personal devotions
and Bible study groups
115 pages, paperback, ISBN 1 870855 40 X

Worship in the Melting Pot
148 pages, paperback, ISBN 1 870855 33 7

Physicians of Souls
The Gospel Ministry
285 pages, paperback, ISBN 1 870855 34 5

Not Like Any Other Book
Interpreting the Bible
161 pages, paperback, ISBN 1 870855 43 4

Do We Have a Policy?
For church health and growth
93 pages, paperback, ISBN 1 870855 30 2

Only One Baptism of the Holy Spirit
109 pages, paperback, ISBN 1 870855 17 5

The Healing Epidemic
227 pages, paperback, ISBN 1 870855 00 0

The Charismatic Phenomenon
[co-authored with John C. Whitcomb]
113 pages, paperback, ISBN 1 870855 01 9

Steps for Guidance
184 pages, paperback, ISBN 1 870855 19 1

Biblical Strategies for Witness
126 pages, paperback, ISBN 1 870855 18 3

Should Christians Drink?
112 pages, paperback, ISBN 1 870855 12 4

www.wakemantrust.org

Audio and video sermons of Dr Masters are available free on the
Metropolitan Tabernacle's web site: www.MetropolitanTabernacle.org